DATE DUE

EARTHWISE

Our Planet

Pam Robson

Stargazer Books

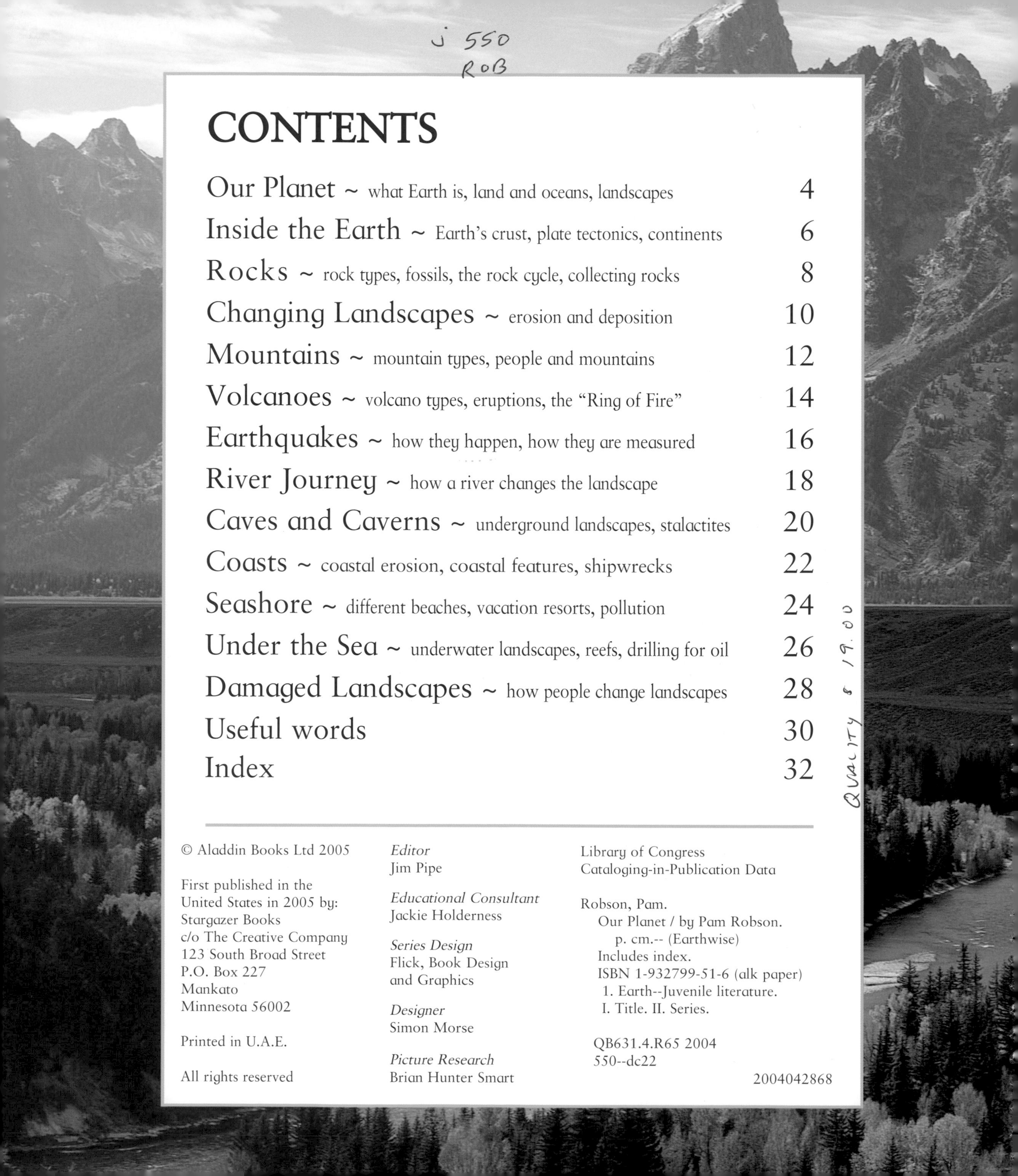

CONTENTS

First published in the
United States in 2005 by:
Stargazer Books
c/o The Creative Company
123 South Broad Street
P.O. Box 227
Mankato
Minnesota 56002

Printed in U.A.E.

Editor
Jim Pipe

Educational Consultant
Jackie Holderness

Series Design
Flick, Book Design
and Graphics

Designer
Simon Morse

Picture Research
Brian Hunter Smart

Library of Congress
Cataloging-in-Publication Data

Robson, Pam.
Our Planet / by Pam Robson.
p. cm.-- (Earthwise)
Includes index.
ISBN 1-932799-51-6 (alk paper)
1. Earth--Juvenile literature.
I. Title. II. Series.

QB631.4.R65 2004
550--dc22

2004042868

INTRODUCTION

We live on a rocky planet called Earth. Its surface, the land, is changing all the time. Earthquakes split the ground and volcanoes create new mountains. Wind and water slowly wear away the land. People can also change the land. They dam rivers and tunnel through mountains.

HOW TO USE THIS BOOK

Watch for the symbol of the magnifying glass for tips on looking at the landscape in your area.

The paintbrush boxes contain activities that relate to the shape of the land where you live.

OUR PLANET

From space, our planet looks smooth. But on the ground we can see hills, valleys, and cliffs. All of these make up the surface of the earth—what we call the landscape.

Salty seas and oceans cover much of Earth's surface. Under the water are mountains, hills, and valleys that we cannot see. We only see the shape of the land that is above water.

EARTH

Our planet is a huge rock spinning in space. But when you dig down into the ground, you will find that much of Earth's rocky surface is covered by a layer of soil in which trees and other plants grow.

Soil is made up of tiny pieces of rock. These contain the minerals that plants need to grow. Soil also contains air, water, and rotting plant and animal matter. Another word for soil is earth—which gives us the name for our planet!

Using a Map

Look at maps of the area where you live. Is the landscape flat or hilly? Lines called contours show the height of the land above sea level. Take a walk near your home and see if you can find the hills on the map. Where contour lines are very close together, the hill will be steep.

Our Planet

From space, Earth looks like a shining blue ball because there is so much water on its surface. Clouds swirl around in the atmosphere. The atmosphere is the layer of air that surrounds our planet. Without air, water, and energy from the sun, there would be no life on Earth.

Hills and Valleys—Rivers flow through valleys between hills. The tallest hills are mountains.

Coasts—Where the land meets the sea there may be high cliffs or sandy beaches.

Lowlands and Plains—A flat, gentle landscape often has good soil for farming.

INSIDE THE EARTH

We can see what is on Earth's surface. But if you could dig a hole down to Earth's center, what would you find? No one knows for sure. Scientists try to find out by exploring its different layers. They study rocks, earthquakes, and volcanoes (below).

If Earth could be sliced open, it would be like a giant peach. Its skin, the earth's surface, is called the crust. Below this is the mantle, a layer of hot, sticky rock. Earth's center is called the core. The outer core is red-hot liquid rock, called magma. The inner core is made of solid nickel and iron. It is 100 times hotter than the hottest desert!

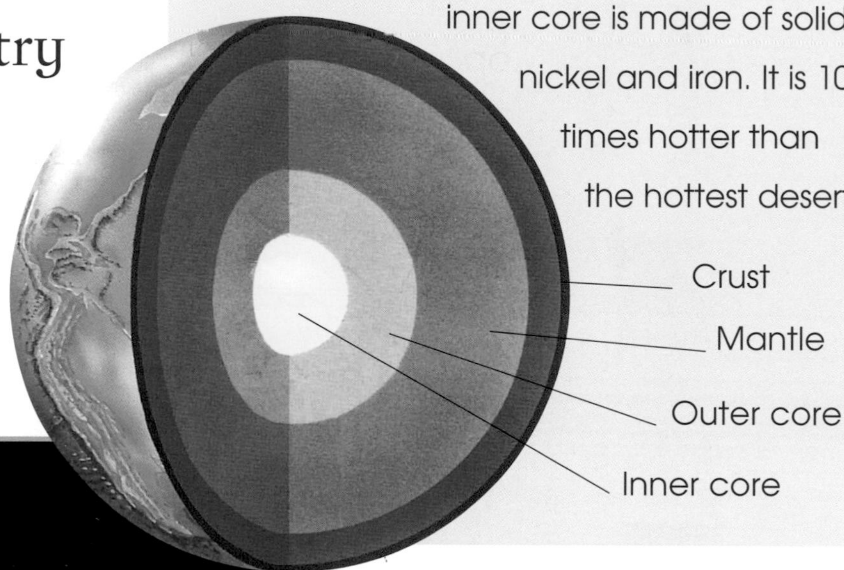

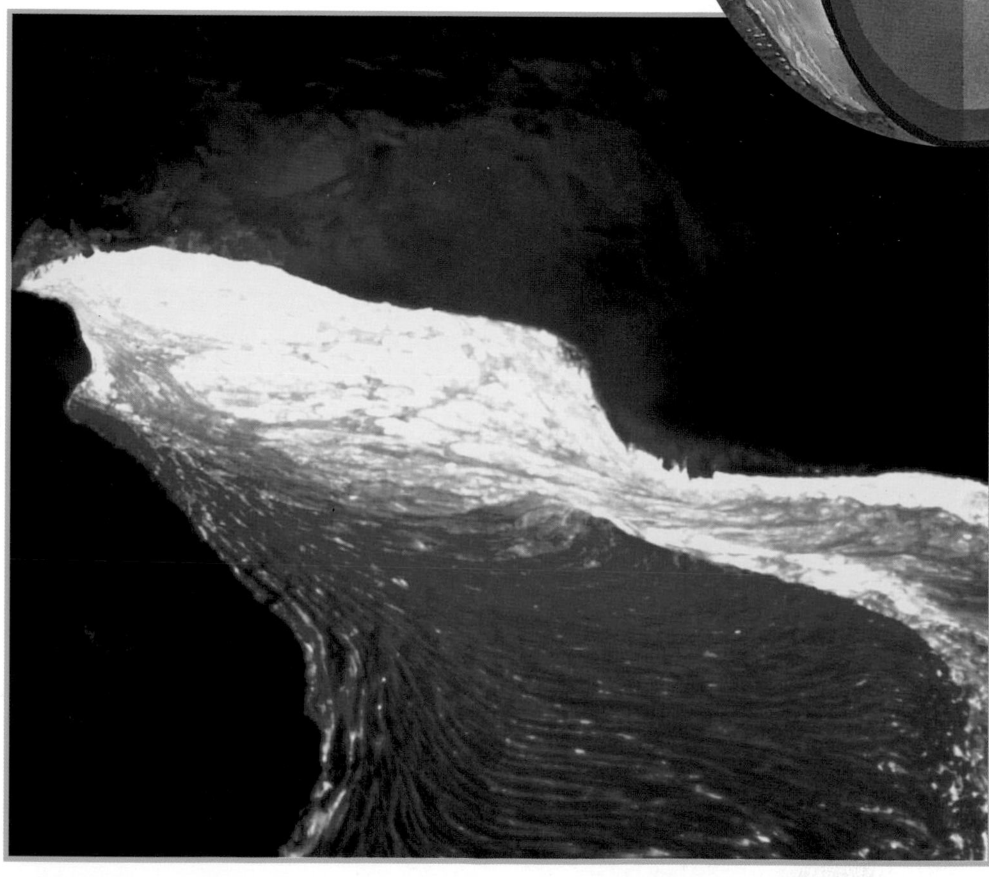

Giant pieces of Earth's crust move around on top of the soft mantle beneath. These moving pieces of crust are called tectonic plates.

When these giant plates push against each other, earthquakes can shake the ground, volcanoes can erupt, and mountains may slowly form.

World Puzzle

Find a world map in an atlas. Photocopy the map and glue it on to cardboard. Cut out the continents of Africa and South America. They almost fit together like puzzle pieces, because they were once joined together.

A very long time ago, the continents were close together in one large piece of land called Pangaea. Over millions of years, the tectonic plates have moved apart. The continents are now separate chunks of land.

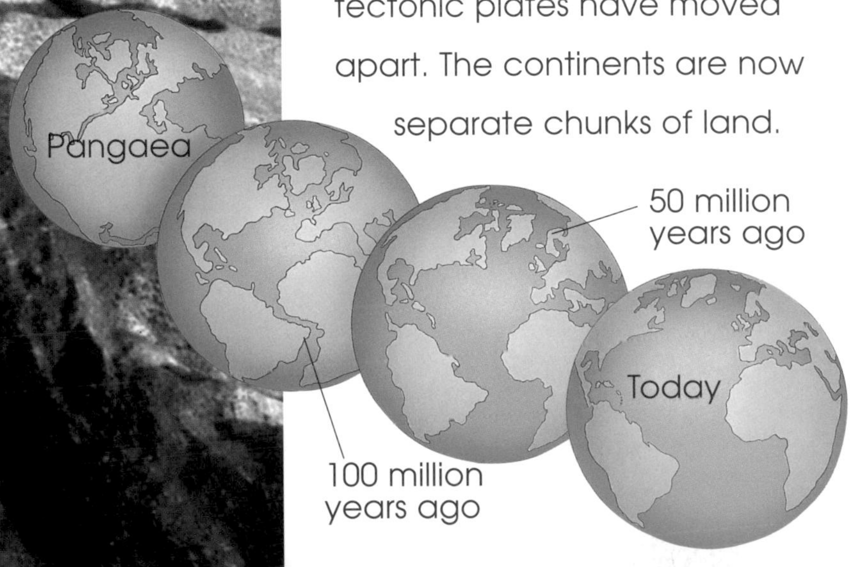

The San Andreas Fault (above) is the place where two tectonic plates meet beneath California. When one of the plates slips suddenly, it can cause an earthquake in the cities of Los Angeles or San Francisco.

ROCKS

Rock is the hard, solid part of Earth's crust. There are many types of rock, which people use in different ways. Granite is a hard rock used in building. It is a type of **igneous** rock. This means it formed when magma from below the ground cooled on the surface. Other rocks, such as marble, form when they are squeezed and pushed deep below the ground. We call them **metamorphic** rocks.

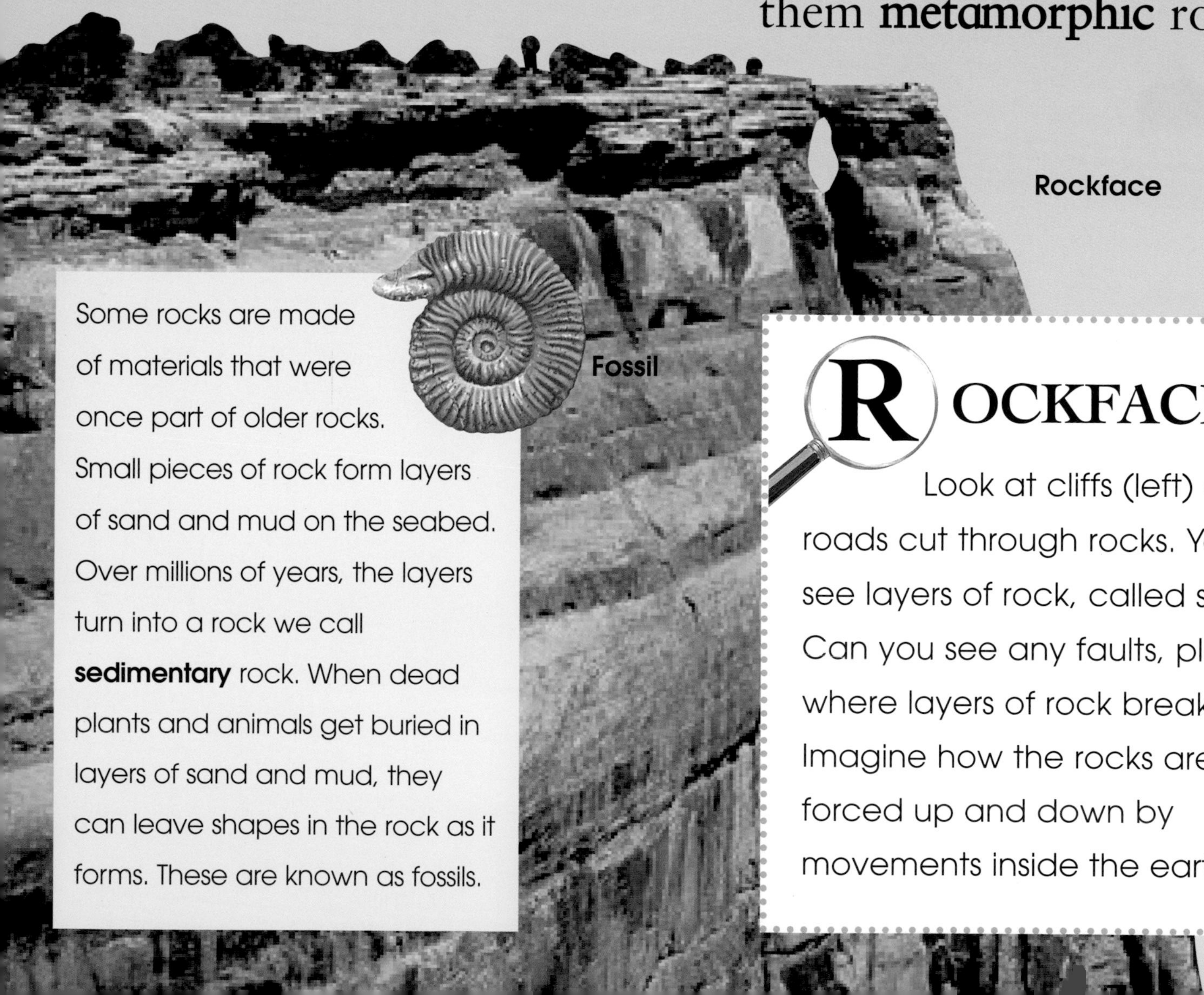

Rockface

Fossil

Some rocks are made of materials that were once part of older rocks. Small pieces of rock form layers of sand and mud on the seabed. Over millions of years, the layers turn into a rock we call **sedimentary** rock. When dead plants and animals get buried in layers of sand and mud, they can leave shapes in the rock as it forms. These are known as fossils.

ROCKFACES

Look at cliffs (left) and roads cut through rocks. You may see layers of rock, called strata. Can you see any faults, places where layers of rock break? Imagine how the rocks are slowly forced up and down by movements inside the earth.

Pebbles

Chalk

Rock Collection

Different rocks are made up of different mixtures of minerals. Some minerals form gemstones, such as rubies, inside the rock. Find out more by making your own collection. Test each sample. Is it very hard, or does it easily crumble like chalk? Does it feel rough or smooth? You can also use a spotter's book to find out the names of your rocks.

The Rock Cycle

Hard rock forms when magma from below the ground cools. This rock is worn away and the grains become sand or mud. These form sedimentary rock. This is forced beneath the surface where it changes again. This new rock is pushed up as magma, or as a mountain. Then the rock cycle begins again.

Rock is worn away by weather (erosion).

Grains of rock form mud or sand (deposition).

Igneous rock forms when hot, liquid rock (magma) is pushed to the surface.

Layers of sand form **sedimentary rock**. This is forced underground.

CHANGING LANDSCAPES

Every hill, cliff, or river near you is always changing. Rocks and soil are worn away by wind, rain, ice, rivers, and waves. This is called erosion. Then the grains of rock are carried to a different place by rivers and streams. This is called deposition.

Mountaintops are shaped by ice.

Cracking Clay

Do your own experiment to see how ice splits rock into smaller pieces. Spray two balls of clay with water. Then wrap them in plastic wrap. Place one ball in the freezer for a day. Then take it out and allow the ice to melt. Repeat this a few more times. Cracks will appear in the frozen clay. But the ball outside the freezer will be unchanged.

When a river reaches the sea, it slows down. The river deposits (leaves behind) mud called silt. The silt mixes with rotting plants and animals from the riverbed. It makes good soil for crops.

In hot deserts and dry, dusty areas, the wind shapes the land. It can create sand dunes in the desert up to 1,000 feet high! Sand blown by the wind also carves strange shapes out of the rocks.

WEARING • AWAY • BUILDINGS

Look at the outside of your home or school. Can you see where the weather is wearing away the stone or brick? Look also for rotting wood, flaky paint, or rusty metal. This erosion takes many years. But car and truck fumes add chemicals to the rain. This causes acid rain, which wears away buildings faster.

MOUNTAINS

Have you ever seen a long line of mountains? This is called a mountain range. Mountain ranges are created by huge forces under the ground. Some are made by volcanoes. Other mountains form when tectonic plates bump into each other. They are like giant "wrinkles" in the rocks.

Mountain Scenes

Mountains are very beautiful, so many artists like to paint mountain scenes. J.M.W. Turner painted this stunning picture of the Alps. Paint your own picture of a mountain scene. Try to show how high your mountain is by painting the clouds at the top of the mountain.

In countries like Portugal (above), farmers grow crops even on mountain slopes. A series of level steps is built around the slope. Each step, or terrace, is separated from the next by a wall. This stops water from running down the slope.

Mountain climbers enjoy trying to reach the top of a mountain, called the summit. As you go up a mountain, it becomes colder and there is less air to breathe. Some mountain tops are so high, they are covered in snow all year round.

Hotels and resorts are built in snow-covered mountain regions. Tourists travel on special railroads that can travel up steep mountain slopes. Cablecars carry skiers to the top of the mountain. People slide down the slopes on snowboards (above) or skis.

Engineers build tunnels through mountains for roads and railroads. They use explosives to blow holes in the rock. Then machines take away the rock pieces. Tunnels make journeys shorter and faster. One of the longest railroad tunnels is the Simplon Tunnel in the Alps, which is 12 miles long.

When a volcano is likely to erupt, we say that it is active. For example, Mount Etna on the island of Sicily erupts regularly. Mount Fuji in Japan (right) has not erupted for a very long time. We say that it is dormant.

VOLCANOES

A volcano starts as a hole in the earth's crust. Hot liquid rock from deep below the ground forces itself through the crack. The volcano erupts (bursts out). It can shoot ash, gas, or hot rock high into the air. After many eruptions, a volcanic mountain may form.

RING • OF • FIRE

Volcanoes often occur where two tectonic plates meet. Look in an atlas to locate Earth's "Ring of Fire" volcanoes (right). They are found in a ring around the edge of the Pacific Ocean. Their cone-shaped peaks stick out above the water. Other volcanoes to look for are Mount St. Helens in Oregon, Stromboli and Vesuvius in Italy, and Pinatubo in the Philippines.

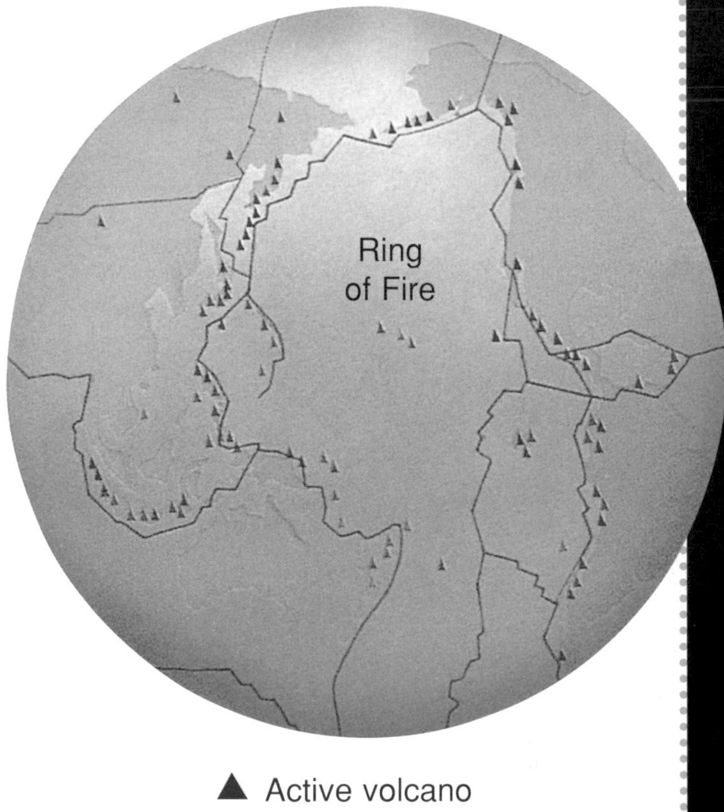

Another group of volcanoes lies in the Atlantic Ocean. The island of Surtsey rose from the sea after one of these volcanoes erupted in 1963.

Mount Kilimanjaro in Tanzania is Africa's highest mountain. It is an extinct volcano. This means that it will never erupt again.

EARTHQUAKES

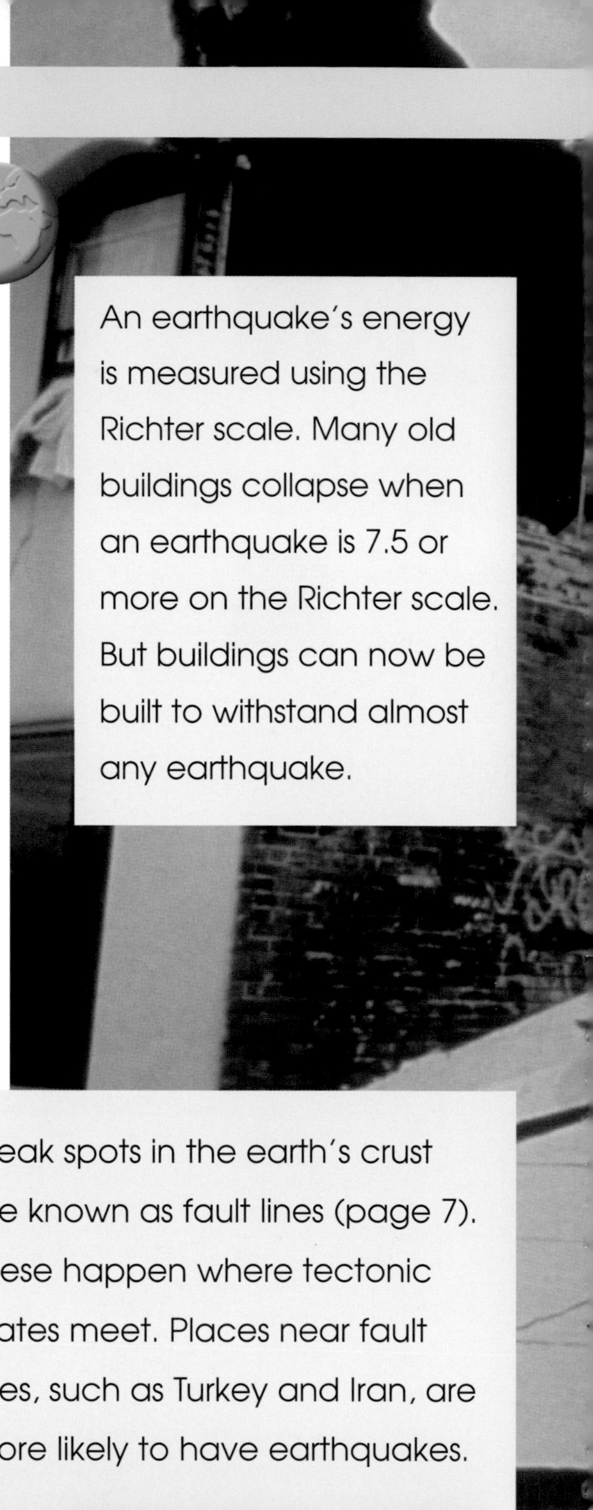

If you stand up on a moving bus, it can feel like the floor is rocking. When an earthquake happens, the ground below shakes, too. Most earthquakes happen in places where tectonic plates meet.

When a tectonic plate moves suddenly, it causes huge vibrations in the ground. We call this an earthquake. It can make trees, buildings, and bridges fall down.

An earthquake's energy is measured using the Richter scale. Many old buildings collapse when an earthquake is 7.5 or more on the Richter scale. But buildings can now be built to withstand almost any earthquake.

MOVING • EARTH

After an earthquake, the shape of the land is changed. Huge cracks appear in the ground (left). Rocks split open. You may see signs of smaller earth movements in your area. If you live near a cliff, you may see the effect of a landslide. Rocks, soil, and trees slide down the hill.

Weak spots in the earth's crust are known as fault lines (page 7). These happen where tectonic plates meet. Places near fault lines, such as Turkey and Iran, are more likely to have earthquakes.

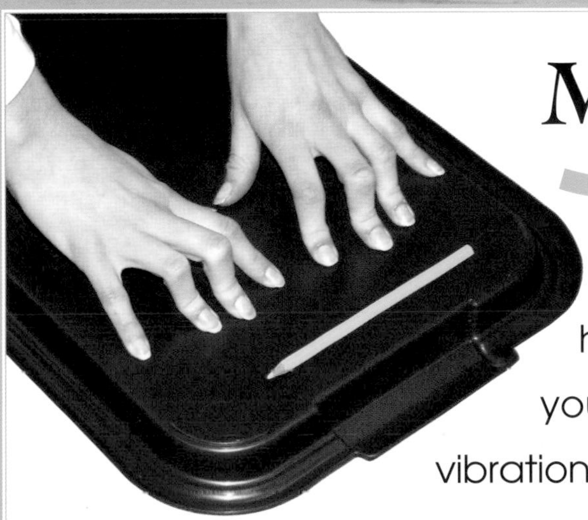

Make an Earthquake

Put a pencil on the table in front of you. Push hard down and forward on the table. Then allow your hand to slip forward suddenly. This creates vibrations, like an earthquake, making the pencil shake.

A stream rushes downhill. It cuts a narrow valley with steep sides. This is in the shape of the letter "V."

RIVER JOURNEY

Rivers also shape the landscape around you. See how channels form if you trickle water from the top of a mound of sand. Rivers usually begin in the hills or mountains. Some rivers begin as melting water from a mass of ice called a glacier. Others begin as springs that bubble out of the ground.

Sticks Game

See how the water flows fastest on the outside of a river bend. Play a game by dropping sticks into a stream. Observe the path taken by each stick. What happens on the bends? Does the water move faster there?

DO NOT GO NEAR WATER WITHOUT AN ADULT.

Waterfalls form when soft rock is worn away.

A large river in a U-shaped valley

As it flows downhill, a stream is joined by rainwater and water from other streams. It becomes a wide river and slows down. The river wears away the valley sides. This makes the valley the shape of a letter "U."

SPRING • WATER

Look in your local supermarket for bottles of spring water. Read the labels to find out where the water comes from. Why do you think spring water is good for you? Think of the minerals the water picks up as it flows over rocks.

The river bends get larger.

As the river gets closer to the sea, the bends get larger. On the inside of each bend, the water flows so slowly that silt (mud) is deposited. On the outside of a bend, it wears away the river bank.

By the time a river reaches the sea, it is very wide and moves very slowly. All the silt carried in the river is deposited close to the river mouth. Silt from a large river may form a delta where the river joins the sea. Silt makes good soil for growing crops such as rice.

The river reaches the sea.

DO NOT ENTER CAVES WITHOUT AN ADULT

CAVES AND CAVERNS

Below our feet is a dark, damp landscape we rarely see. Limestone rock has lots of cracks that allow rainwater to seep (leak) through the rock. Over millions of years, the water wears away the rock. It can form networks of caves and passages. Amazing stalactites hang from cave ceilings. Stalagmites point upward from the floor.

CAVE • VISIT

Look at a map of your local area. Are there any caves in your area that are open to visitors?

In many parts of the world, you can visit spectacular caves. Many caves have underground lakes, rivers, and waterfalls. Paths and electric lights allow visitors to explore the caves safely.

C ORAL • REEFS

Coral reefs are a very colorful part of the ocean. Reefs are found in warm, shallow seas close to shore. They provide homes and food for many plants and animals. If you can, watch one of the many TV programs about reefs. Learn about the fish, crabs, turtles, and other animals that live on a coral reef.

Scientists have found tall volcanic chimneys (above) on the ocean floor. The chimneys are called Black Smokers because they release hot, black fumes. These make the water very hot. Only a few animals, like this crab, can live in the hot, poisonous water nearby.

Fossil fuels like coal, oil, and gas have been used by people for a long time. Smoke from these fuels has polluted the air. This traps heat from the sun and may be why the earth is getting warmer.

DAMAGED LANDSCAPE

People make huge changes to the shape of the land. They dig deep mines and quarries. They build high dams across rivers. They tunnel deep into mountains. Forests are cut down and garbage is buried beneath the ground. Our pollution is changing the earth's climate. Desert areas are spreading and sea levels are rising.

GARBAGE • DUMPS

You probably don't have to look very hard to find garbage in your area. People produce lots of it! Some garbage is buried under the ground in places called landfills. But trash is also put in open dumps. These dumps can ruin the natural beauty of the landscape.

Trash ruins any landscape (right), including your local streets!

In China, there is a huge desert called the Gobi Desert. This desert has been growing bigger every year. One reason for this is that people have cut down forests nearby. To protect the city of Beijing from Gobi sandstorms, trees have been planted close to the city.

When people cut down forests it makes a big change to the landscape. When there are no trees, the soil is easily washed away by rain and wind.

Take Action

Are you worried about your local landscape? Perhaps there are plans to build a road through an ancient forest. Ask your teacher or parent to help you write a letter to your local council. Explain why you enjoy the landscape as it is.

Dams have been built across many large rivers. They use the power of falling water to make electricity. When a dam is built, it creates a lake behind it. This changes the shape of the land forever. Dams can destroy animal homes. People may also be forced to leave their homes.

USEFUL WORDS

atmosphere—the thick layer of air that surrounds Earth.

contours—lines drawn on a map that join places the same height above sea level.

delta—land at the place where a large river enters the sea, formed by silt from the river.

deposition—when grains of rock are carried to a different place by rivers and streams.

dissolve—to make something liquid, often by putting it into liquid. Sugar dissolves in hot water.

Earth's core—the solid metal center of our planet.

Earth's crust—the rocky outer surface of Earth.

erosion—the wearing away of the land by natural forces such as wind or rain.

fault—a break in Earth's crust, where rocks are pushed up or down.

fossil—(left) the rocky remains or traces of an ancient animal or plant.

groin—a barrier built across a beach to stop sand or stones from moving.

landscape—our view of the land.

magma—(right) hot, liquid rock from below the earth's crust.

mantle—the part of Earth below the crust and outside the core.

silt—the fine mud that settles at the bottom of rivers. It is made up of tiny pieces of rock.

soil—a mix of minerals, tiny pieces of rock, dead plant and animal matter, air, and water.

stalactites/stalagmites—the icicle shapes formed when limestone dissolves in rainwater. Stalactites hang from the roof of caves, stalagmites grow from the floor.

tectonic plates—giant pieces of Earth's crust. They move slowly on top of the soft mantle below.

Find Out More

Take a look at these books & websites:

Books: Earthwise: Water (Stargazer Books); Geography for Fun: Mountains and Our Moving Earth (Stargazer Books)

Websites: http://volcano.und.nodak.edu
http://earthquake.usgs.gov/4kids
http://mineral.galleries.com/default.htm

STORY • TIME

Watch for the many myths and legends that explain the landscape. In Hawaii, some people say that when the volcano Kilauea erupts it is a sign that the goddess Pele is angry. In Japan, people once believed that earthquakes happened when the big catfish that lived inside the earth moved about.

INDEX

Photocredits

Abbreviations: l-left, r-right, b-bottom, t-top, c-center, m-middle

Front cover tl, tr, bl & br, back cover, 2-3, 5bl, 5bm, 5br, 9mlb, 24bl, 28bl, 28br, 29mr, 29bl, 30tr — Photodisc. Front cover c, 27mr — Stockbyte. Front cover inset, 28ml — Comstock. 1, 6bl, 9bl, 10tr, 11t, 13tr, 13ml, 13br, 14-15, 15 both, 31bl, 32b — Digital Stock. 3b, 18mr, 19br, 24c, 24mr — Argentinian Embassy, London. 4-5, 9lmt, 10br, 25tr, 30-31 — Corbis. 7l, 9br — R. E. Wallace; USGS. 7tr — Brand X Pictures. 8-9 — US National Park Service. 9tl, 25l, 27 main, 27bm — NOAA. 9mr, 12-13, 12bl, 12mr, 14t, 18tl, 18br, 20-21, 20bm, 21t, 21ml, 22 both, 23 both, 29tl, 29br — Corel. 10bl, 17bl, 21br — Select Pictures. 11br, 19tr — PBD. 16bl, 16br, 17t — FEMA. 19ml — US Fish & Wildlife Service. 19bm — John Deere. 24tl — Scott Bauer; ARS. 26ml — Brian Moore; USCG.